Meet and Greet

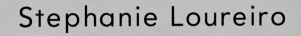

Stephanie Loureiro

It is nice to say hello.

How do you greet someone?

I smile.

They high five.

We talk.

Think and Talk

How does greeting someone make you feel?

They say hello.

They say hello too.

How do you say hello?

Jump into
Fiction

Greetings

Hello. I am Mike.

It is nice to meet you.

LIB

Civics in Action

We say hi to friends. We wave and smile. We meet new people too. We say hello.

1. Think about meeting a new person.

2. Think about how you greet them.

3. Draw a picture. Show what you will do when you meet a new person.